The Blueprint to Python Programming

A Beginners Guide: Everything You Need to Know to Get Started

By: CyberPunk Architects

Introduction

There are many people who are interested in getting into the world of coding. They want to learn some of the basics so that they can work on their own programs, learn how to work more on their own computers, or even get started on doing work for other people. But there are many different coding languages that you can learn to work with and sometimes this can be confusing to learn which is right for you. This guidebook is going to spend some time talking about the Python coding language, one of the best languages to learn as a beginner for its ease of use as well as all its power.

In this guidebook, you are going to learn about the Python coding language. We will start with some of the basics, including learning how to install the software, as well as the right IDE and text editor so that you are able to write some of your own code. We will then move on to some of the basics of this language that you would like to include inside your codes to make them work the best. And then we move on to handling the exceptions in Python, working with loops to get a block of code to repeat without having to rewrite it a bunch of times, and the conditional statements that will make decisions for you regardless of the answer that your user places into the code.

The Python language is one of the easiest coding languages to learn how to use. It is designed for the beginner with all of the power that you are looking for inside a new coding language. This guidebook is going to take some time to help you as a beginner learn more about coding with this language so you can create some of your own codes and really join the coding community.

Chapter 1: Getting to Know the Python Program

Getting started with a new programming language can be a bit scary. You want to make sure that you are picking out one that is easy to use so that you can understand what is going on inside of the program. But you may also have some big dreams of what you want to accomplish with the programming and want an option that is able to keep up with that. The good news is that the Python programming language is able to help with all of this and is the perfect coding language for a beginner to get started with.

There are many reasons why you would enjoy working with the Python language. It is easy to learn, is meant for beginners, and it works with some of the other coding languages that you may want to learn to add in more power. It is based on the English language so there are not going to be too many issues with learning difficult words, and it has a lot of the power that you need without all the complicated make-up of other coding languages. As you will see in a minute, the syntax in Python is really easy to learn and there are a lot of powerful things that you can do with this coding language, even as a beginner.

The Python library is going to be a great help to you as you get started with this language. It has many of the syntaxes and examples that you need to help you out when you get stuck or when you have some issues figuring out how to complete some steps in Python. The community with this coding language is large as well, due to the fact that this is an easy code to work with and is great for beginners, so you will be able to find others to ask questions of or you can read through forums to learn more about the projects you want to work on.

If you are interested in getting started with the Python language, there are a few things that you will need to have on hand to make the process easier. First, you will need to make sure that the right text editor is in place on your computer. This is important because it is the software that you need to use in order to write out the codes to use inside of Python. The text editor doesn't have to be high end or complicated, and in fact, using the free Notepad option on any Windows computer, or another of this nature, will work just fine.

Once you have chosen the text editor that you would like to use, you will be able to download the actual Python program to use. The nice thing about this is that Python is free to download, as is the IDE and the other options that you will need, so you won't have to worry about the financial aspect of it. To get the Python program set up, you will just need to visit the Python website and choose the version that you would like to use.

While you are getting the Python program set up on your computer, you will also need to make sure that you download the IDE in the same instance. The IDE is basically the environment that you are going to be working in, and it will include the compiler that you need to interpret the codes that you are writing. It is often best to use the one that comes with the Python programming because this one is designed to work the best, but if you are used to working with a different IDE, you will be able to use that one as well.

If you find that there are times that you have questions about using this coding language, such as how to work on a particular code or if you are lost about why something isn't working, you should take the time to visit a Python community. The Python language has been around for some time, and it is one of the most popular coding languages in use, so the communities are pretty large. You should be able to find many groups of beginners and those who are more advanced who will be able to help you with your questions or any of the concerns that you have while learning this language.

Some of the basic parts of the Python code

Now that you have some of the Python software all set up and ready to go, it is time to work on some of the basics that come with this code. There are a lot of different parts that work together to write some amazing codes inside of Python, but learning about these basics will make it a bit easier to handle and when getting into some of the more complex processes later on. Here are some of the basics that we are going to concentrate on first before moving to some of the harder stuff later on:

Keywords

Any coding software that you use is going to have some keywords. These are words that will tell the interpreter what you want to happen in the code, so they are important to be familiar with. It is recommended that you do not use these anywhere else in your code in order to avoid confusion or error when the interpreter gets ahold of it, considering these are major action words. Some of the keywords that you should look at when working in the Python language include:

- False
- Finally
- Class
- Is
- Return

- Continue
- None
- For
- Try
- True
- Lambda
- Def
- Nonlocal
- From
- While
- Global
- Del
- And
- Not
- Raise
- In
- Except
- Break
- Pass
- Yield
- As
- If
- Elif
- Or
- Import
- Assert

- Else
- Import

This is a good list to keep on hand when you are writing your codes. This will help you to send the right information to the interpreter when you are writing through the code. Any time that you see an error message come up after writing out code make sure to check if you used one of those words properly within your statements.

Names of Identifiers

While working on a new code or program with Python, you will need to work with a few different things including variables, functions, entities, and classes. These will all have names that are also called identifiers. When you are creating the name of an identifier, regardless of the type you are working on, some of the rules that you should follow include:

- You should have letters, both lower case and upper casework are acceptable, the underscore symbol, and numbers. You are able to choose any combination of these as well. Just make sure that there are no spaces between characters.
- You can never start an identifier with a number. You are able to use something like "sixdogs," but "6dogs" would not be acceptable.

- The identifier should not be one of the keywords that were listed above, and there should never be one of the keywords inside of it.

If you do go against one of these rules, you will notice that a syntax error will occur and the program will close on you. In addition to the rules above, you should ensure that the identifiers are easy to read for the human eye. This is important because while the identifier may follow the rules that were set out above, they can still have trouble when the human eye isn't able to understand what you are writing out.

When you are creating your identifier, make sure that you pick one that will be descriptive. Going with one that will describe what the code is doing or what the variable contains is a good place to start. You should also be wary of using abbreviations because these aren't always universally understood and can cause some confusion.

Chapter 2: Some of the Basic Commands You Should Know in Python

In addition to the things that we discussed above pertaining to the Python language, there are some other things that you can put into your codes to make them really strong. There are many options and functions that you can incorporate into the codes in order to do things like: tell other programmers what to do inside the code, add similar parts with the same characteristics together, and so much more. Let's take some time to look at the different commands that you are able to use in your codes with Python and what they all mean.

Comments

Comments are a great thing to know how to use inside of Python. They allow you to leave little notes inside of the code for yourself or for other coders who want to take a look at what you are doing. The compiler is set up to not recognize these comments, this way you are able to put in as many comments as you would like without it affecting how the code is going to execute.

Python makes it really easy to add in these comments. You will simply need to use the "#" sign in front of the comment that you want to leave inside the code. Once you are done with the comment that you want to leave, you just need to hit the return button and start out on a new line so that the compiler knows that you are starting on a new part of the code. As mentioned, you are able to leave as many of these little notes inside of your code as you would like, but try to keep them just to the ones that are needed in order to keep the code looking nice and organized.

Statements

Another thing that you are able to add into your code is statements. Whenever you are working on a code, you will need to leave these statements inside of your code so that the compiler has some idea of what you would like to have shown up on the screen. A statement is going to basically be a unit of code that you can send over to the interpreter. Then your interpreter will look at the statement that you want to use and then execute it based on the command that you are giving it.

When you work on writing the code, you can choose how many statements you are able to write at one time. You can choose to just have one statement that is inside of your code, or you can have several of them based on what you would like to have happen inside of the code. As long as you keep the statements inside of the brackets inside the code and you use all the correct rules when you are writing out that part of the code, you will be able to include as many of these statements as needed into the code.

When you choose to add in a statement (or more than one statement) into the code, you will send it through to the interpreter, which is then going to work to execute the commands that you want, just as long as you make sure that you put everything else in the right place. The results of your statements will then show up on the screen when you execute it, and you can always go back in and make changes or adjustments as needed. Let's look at an example of how this would work when using statements in your code:

```
x = 56
Name = John Doe
z = 10

print(x)
print(Name)
print(z)
```

When you send this over to the interpreter, the results that should show up on the screen are:

It is as simple as that. Open up Python and give it a try to see how easy it is to just get a few things to show up in your interpreter.

Working with variables

Variables are a good thing to learn about the inside of the Python code because they can be used to store your code in specific parts of your computer. So basically, you will find these variables are just spots on the memory of your computer that will be reserved for the values of the code that you are working on. When you are working on the variables in the code, you are telling the computer to save some room on its memory to store these variables. Depending on what type of data you would like to use in the code, the variable is able to tell the computer what space should be saved on that location.

Giving the variable a value

In order to make the variables work inside the code, you need to make sure that they get a value assigned to each. Otherwise they are just basic places on the memory. You need to put some kind of value to the variable in order to get it to work properly, so it reacts inside the code. There are two types of variables that you will be able to use, and the one that you choose will determine the value type that you give to it. The different types of variables that we can pick from include:

Float: this would include numbers like 3.14 and so on.
String: this is going to be like a statement where you could write out something like "Thank you for visiting my page!" or another similar phrase.
Whole number: this would be any of the other numbers that you would use that do not have a decimal point.

When you are using this program, you will not need to use declarations in order to reserve this space on the memory since this is something that will occur right when you add a value to the variable you are working with. If you want to make sure that this is going to happen automatically, you just need to use the (=) symbol so that the value knows which variable it is supposed to be working with:

Some examples of how this works include:

x = 12   *#this is an example of an integer assignment*
pi = 3.14   *#this is an example of a floating point assignment*

customer name = John Doe   *#this is an example of a*
string assignment

Now at this point, we are looking at just writing the code, but what if you would like to have the interpreter execute the code that we are using. Luckily, this is pretty simple to work on. You just need to make sure that you write out the word "print" before the statement that you want to use. However, in the newer versions, such as Python 3, you would want to add in the parenthesis. Either way, this is pretty easy to learn how to do. Here is a good example of how you would be able to make this work inside Python:

print(x)
print(pi)
print(customer name)

Based on the information listed above, when this is printed out, your interpreter is going to execute the results:

12

3.14
John Doe

You are also able to add in more than one value to the same variable if this is what needs to happen for the code to work within your code. You just need to make sure that you are including the equal sign ("=") in between each of the parts to make it work the right way. For example, "a = b = c = 1" would be acceptable and makes it so that all of those variables would equal 1 inside of your code. This is just a simpler option to use rather than writing each of these out on their own and making them equal to 1.

These are just a few more of the basics that you will need to learn how to use when it comes to writing out your own codes in Python. These are pretty simple to learn how to do and you are going to enjoy all the power that they add into even the simplest codes you will be writing in the beginning.

Chapter 3: Working with Loops in Python

Now that we know some of the basics associated with working on the Python language, it is time to move into some of the more complex parts of this language and learn how to make it all work for your program. With the other options included in this guidebook, we talk about decision control instructions or sequential control instructions. When we are working with the decision control options (which will be discussed in the following chapter), we are putting the calculations into a fixed order to be figured out. With the sequential option, the interpreter is going to execute your instructions based on how your conditions will turn up at the end. There are a few limitations that come up with these options, mostly because they are only able to do the action once.

Now, what happens if you would like to have the action done more than once? With the other options that we discussed in this book, this would mean that you would need to rewrite the code over and over again until it is repeated as many times as you would like it to be. But what happens when you want to make something like a table that counts from 1 to

100? Do you want to write out the same part of code 100 times to make this happen?

Luckily, there are some options within Python that can be used to make it easier to write out these things as many times as you would like, while only taking up a few lines. These are called "loops," and they ensure that you are able to repeat the code as many times as you would like, from one to a thousand or higher if you would like. They are much easier to write out, they can save you a lot of time, and they will basically ensure that you are going to get the loop to continue until the conditions of the code are no longer true.

At first, you may feel that these loops are going to be kind of complicated because you have to tell the program how to repeat itself over and over as many times as you want, but it is actually pretty simple. There are three different types of loops that you can use inside of Python depending on what you would like the code to do. The three loops that you are able to use include the "while" loop, the "for" loop, and the "nesting" loop. Each of the loops is going to work in a different way to help you to repeat the part of the code that you need as many times as needed. Let's take a look at how each of these work, and when you would choose to use each one inside of your code.

What is the while loop?

The first loop that we are going to take a look at is the while loop. This is a good one to start on when you would like to make the code repeat itself, or go through the same actions, a fixed amount of times. For example, if you want to make sure that the loop goes through the same steps ten times, you would want to use the while loop. But if you would like to use this to create an indefinite number of loops, this is not the option to go with.

One of the examples that you would want to use with the while loop is when calculating out the amount of interest that is owed or paid. You can do this several times in order to find the perfect option for your user, but this one can be set up so that the user will not have to go back through the program multiple times and get frustrated. Here is a good example that you can use in order to learn how the while loop statements are going to work when you would like to calculate simple interest:

#calculation of simple interest. Ask user to input principal, rate of interest, number of years.

counter = 1
while(counter <= 3):
        principal = int(input("Enter the principal amount:"))

numberofyeras = int(input("Enter the number of years:"))

rateofinterest = float(input("Enter the rate of interest:"))

simpleinterest = principal * numberofyears * rateofinterest/100

print("Simple interest = %.2f" %simpleinterest)

#increase the counter by 1

counter = counter + 1

print("You have calculated simple interest for 3 time!")

With this particular loop, the user will be able to put in the numbers they want to use for interest three times. After they are done, it will be set up to have a message show up on the screen. You can make this more complicated if you would like, adding in more lines for the user to input their answer as many times as they choose. The user of the program will be the one in charge, choosing how much they want to put into each of the spots. The user will be able to redo this program as well, starting over at the beginning, if they would like to add in more than the three interest spots than what they have in right now.

Working with the for loop

Now that we understand a bit more about the while loop, it is time to move on to the for loop. This one will work similarly to the other loop, but is a more traditional way to work with loops. If you have worked in any other coding languages in the past, you may be more familiar with this particular loop. If you do plan to use Python with another coding language, you should consider using the for loop to make things easier.

When using the for loop, the user will not be the one who defines the conditions that will make the loop stop. The Python program is going to make the statement continue repeating, in the exact order that it is placed inside your statement. Below you will find an example of how the for loop would work inside your code:

```
# Measure some strings:
words = ['apple', 'mango', 'banana', 'orange']
for w in words:
print(w, len(w))
```

Take some time to insert these statements into your compiler. With this one, the four fruits that are in this code, or the other statements that you choose to use, will repeat in the order that you write them out. If you are writing out this particular code and you want to make sure that they come out in a different order than what is listed above, you will need to make sure that you turn them around when writing the code. The computer will not take the time to make the changes and it is not going to allow you to change these at all when you are working on the actual code.

On the other hand, if you are looking for the loop to just go through a certain sequence of numbers or words, such as only wanting the first three fruits to show up on the screen, you will find that using your range() function is the best one for this. This function is going to generate a big list of the arithmetic progressions that you can use inside of the code to help make this easier.

The nested loops

The third type of loop that we are going to take a look at is the nested loop. This one is going to sound a bit more complicated than you are used to with the other two options, but the code is actually going to be shorter than the others, and all the options that you are going to be able to do with the nested loop can make it a great one to learn even as a beginner. To keep things basic, the nested loop is just a loop that is inside of another loop. Both of the loops will just keep going through the repeat process until both of the programs have time to finish.

We are going to take a moment to look at an example of working on the nested loops. We are going to use the idea of a multiplication table in order to show you how several loops inside your code will be able to bring up a lot of information and you will only need to have a few lines of code to make this happen. The code that we are going to write will make the multiplication table go from 1 up to 10. Here is the example that you are able to use:

#write a multiplication table from 1 to 10
For x in xrange(1, 11):
      For y in xrange(1, 11):

*Print '%d = %d' % (x, y, x*x)*

When you get the output of this program, it is going to look similar to this:

1*1 = 1

1*2 = 2

1*3 = 3

1*4 = 4

1*5 = 5

This would continue going until you got all the way up to

1*10 = 2

Then it would move on to do the table by twos such as this:

2*1 =2

2*2 = 4

2*3 = 6

For this one, you are going to keep on going until you end up with 10*10 and the answer that goes with this. You will have a complete multiplication table without having to write out the lines that go with each one, which makes this whole process easier to handle. Just look at the code above, there are only four lines (one of which is a comment), and you can get a table that is pretty complete and long. This is just one of the samples of what you are able to do and one of the main reasons that people will choose to go with loops rather than trying to write out all of the lines that they need.

Loops are one of the best things that you can work on when it comes to being inside the Python language. It can simplify the code that you are working on and ensures that you are able to get a lot of stuff done inside the code without having too much information written out and making it look like a mess. Try out a few of these loop options in your code and see what a difference they can make.

Chapter 4: Handling Exceptions in Your Code

There are times when you will need to work with exceptions when working inside the code. These can work one of two ways. For the first one, it is an exception that the program doesn't like, such as trying to divide a number by zero. When this happens, an error is going to come up on the screen, but you will be able to change the message that comes up on the screen with this to help avoid issues and to make sure that your user has some idea of what the issue is. Then there are exceptions that are particular to your program. If you do not want to allow your user to put in a certain number or another input, you would want to raise an exception to make this not allowed.

So any time that you would like to show the user that a condition is considered abnormal within the code, you will want to bring out the exceptions. There are several types of these that show up inside of the code, and some of which are as simple as writing out the code the wrong way or using the incorrect spelling that will cause the errors.

Any time that you are working in your Python program, and you want to make sure that you are bringing up the exceptions in the proper way, you will want to check out the Python library. There are several of these exceptions that are already in place inside the library and will save you a lot of time. It can be extremely beneficial when you check these exceptions out first. There are several exception types that you are able to use inside this language, including whenever you are dividing a number by zero, or whenever you try to reach a part that is outside the end of the file.

Exceptions can be a nice thing to work with within Python. The nice thing is that you aren't stuck dealing with the error messages that come up on a code. You can change them up a bit to help explain what is going on to the user so that any confusion can be bypassed. When an error message comes up on the screen, it can be difficult to determine what is wrong, especially if your user has no experience working with coding at all. But when you can make some changes, such as adding in a message like "you are trying to divide by zero!" it can explain what is going on with the error so the user can correct or change their process, and makes your code a bit more user-friendly.

You are also able to make some of your own exceptions if the code you are writing asks for it. You will not be able to find these inside of the Python library, but it is still an option that you are able to use. You will need to create some of these on your own so that an error, which can be a message like you did with the ones that were found in the library, will make things easier for the user to understand why the error is showing up.

When you are trying to write out exceptions within the Python language, there are a few things that you are going to find inside of your Python library in which you should take a bit of time to look over and learn how to work with. If you would like to work on the exceptions, you will need to make sure that you learn some of the key terms that need to be present to tell the compiler what you are doing. There are many options to choose from, but some of the statements that are best for working inside of your code with exceptions inside of Python coding include:

- Finally: with this one, you will be able to bring up the word to do the cleanup actions. This is a good one to use whether the user brings up the exception or not.
- Assert: this is the condition that is used whenever you would like to trigger that an exception has occurred inside the code.
- Try/except: these are the keywords that you will want to use whenever you are trying out a block of code. It is going to be recovered because of the exception that

was raised either by you or by the Python program for some other reason.

- Raise: when you use the raise command, you are working to trigger the exception outside the code, doing so manually.

These are some of the best words to use in order to work with your exceptions and to make sure also that you will get all of your errors and other parts to work within the code. Whether you want to raise an exception that is recognized by the code or you are trying to work with one that is just for your program, in particular, you will be able to use these to help make things work within the code.

Raising an exception

Now that we have taken some time to look at what exceptions are all about, it is now time to learn how to raise exceptions. This is a pretty easy concept for you to work on and understand. For example, whenever you are working with the code inside of Python, and there is some kind of issue that is coming up with it, or you see that the program is trying to do things that aren't allowed within the rules of Python, the compiler is going to raise an exception for the behavior in question. This is because the program is going to see the issue and will not be sure about how it should react.

In some cases, the exception that is going to be raised will be pretty simple and could be something like naming the code the wrong way or spelling something wrong. You will just need to go back through the code and make the changes. Or there could even be some issues with the user attempting an action that is not allowed by the code, such as when a user may try to divide by zero. Let's take a look at how this is going to work so that you can see the steps that are needed in order to raise an exception:

x = 10

y = 10

result = x/y #trying to divide by zero

print(result)

The output that you are going to get when you try to get the interpreter to go through this code would be:

>>>

Traceback (most recent call last):

   File "D: \Python34\tt.py", line 3, in <module>

   result = x/y

ZeroDivisionError: division by zero

>>>

For the example that we did above, the Python coding language is going to show an error because you were trying to take a number and divide it by zero. The Python language is one that won't allow you to do this action, and so the error is going to come up on the screen. As we mentioned above, when you see that this error is coming up, the user may be confused and not understand what is going on at all. When you use this to raise up an exception, you should consider changing up the message so that the user has some idea of what is going on so that he or she can make the correct and necessary changes so that the code will work the way that it should.

How to make your own exceptions

So far, we have spent most of our time looking at the steps that you will need to take in order to work with the exceptions that are already recognized by the system. But what happens when you would like to raise some of your own exceptions that work with your particular program that the system does not already recognize? A good example for this is when you want to make sure that your user is not able to place specific numbers into the system. You want to make sure that when the user places these numbers into the system, they are going to get an exception. Or if you would like the user to put in five numbers and they only put in four, you could use the idea of exceptions as well.

The trick with this type of action is that the Python program may not see that there is even an issue. The program is not going to realize that there is an issue with just putting in four numbers rather than the five unless you tell it that this is an issue. You will be the one who is able to set up the exceptions that you want to use, and you can mess around and add in any exception that you would like as long as it meets up with the other rules that are used inside of Python. Let's take a look at the example that is below so that we can understand how the exceptions work and to get some practice with using these:

```
class CustomException(Exception):
def_init_(self, value):
        self.parameter = value
def_str_(self):
        return repr(self.parameter)


try:
        raise CustomException("This is a CustomError!")
except CustomException as ex:
        print("Caught:", ex.parameter)
```

When you use this syntax, you will get the message of "Caught: This is a CustomError!" and any time that your user is on the program and puts in the wrong information, the error message is going to show up. This error is going to be caught if you put the conditions into the program the right way and it is important, especially if you set up your own exceptions in the code, that you place the conditions into the code.

It is possible to add in any wording as you would like into this part, so you can change it up as much as you would like to help better explain to the user what the error message means or what they may be doing wrong.. Mess around with this a little bit and you will find that it is easier than ever to set up some of your own exceptions or deal with the exceptions that are going on inside of your code.

Working with exceptions is a great way to ensure that you are getting the most out of your code. There are times when the code will see an abnormal condition and will need to put up a message or you will be working on your own program, and you will want to make up some of these abnormal conditions to work with what you are doing. Take a look at some of the examples that are done inside of this chapter, and you will be able to work with any of the exceptions that you would like in Python.

Chapter 5: Conditional Statements in Python

When it comes to working with your code, there will be times when you will want to make sure that the code is going to function in a specific way based on the conditions that you set, as well as the answer that the user puts in. You can keep it simple and have only one answer as an output when the user inputs an answer that is considered true based on your conditions, or you can make it more complex so that different answers will come up based on whether the input from the user is true or false. You can also give the user multiple options to input, and they can choose from those. In this chapter, we are going to take some time to talk about the different conditional statements that will work inside the Python code, including the "if" statement, the "if else" statement and the "elif" statements.

The if statement

The first statement that we are going to work with inside of Python is the "if" statement. This is the most basic of the conditional statements, and it is often a good place to start when first learning code. But there will be some challenges when it comes to the user putting in an answer that does not agree with the conditions you set.

With the if statement, you must set the conditions and then the program will do the rest, waiting for the answer from the user. If the user puts in an answer that is considered true, based on the conditions that you set, the rest of the code will be executed. This is usually in the form of a statement of some sort showing up on the screen, and then the compiler moving on to the next part of the code. On the other hand, if the user puts in an answer that is not allowed or is considered false based on the conditions that you set, nothing is going to happen. The if statements are not set up for false answers, so the program will just stop at that point.

There are going to be some issues with this of course, but it is a good place to get started. This one will help you to see how the conditional statements are going to work and gets you some practice with the compiler, but we will look at some conditional statements that are able to look further into the work we are doing so that answers will show up regardless of the answers that are put in. Let's take a look at an example of working with the if statement to give you some practice.

age = int(input("Enter your age:"))
if (age <=18):

print("You are not eligible for voting, try next election!")

print("Program ends")

Let's take a look at this syntax a bit to see what is going on. With this one, when the user comes onto the site and says that their age is under 18, they will match as true with the conditions that you set. This means that the statement that you put in, the "You are not eligible for voting, try next election!", will come up on the screen.

On the other hand, if the user puts in that they are another age, such as 25, into this code, nothing is going to happen. The if statement is not set up in order to handle this issue and there are no statements that are going to show up if this situation occurs. The compiler will just stop working on the code because it is false. You will need to make some changes to the code to handle this.

For the most part, you are not going to be able to use this type of conditional statement. The user is not wrong if they enter an age that is above 18 in the example above and they aren't going to really care for it if they can't see any results after they enter their age. How would you feel if you put in an answer to a program and it just stopped? The if statement is not the most efficient method of taking care of your conditional statements, so there will be many times that you should avoid using this at all. That is where the if else statement is going to come in handy.

If else statement

As we talked about above, there are some issues that come up when using the if statement. If your user enters an answer that is considered true with the if statement, the correct part of the code will execute. But if your user enters an answer that is seen as false (even if it is true for them), they will end up with a blank screen. This can easily end up with some problems when working within your code.

This is when the if else statement is going to come in use. With this one, you are able to set up true and false conditions, and different parts of the code are going to be executed based on the answers that the user gives. Pertaining to the prior example, the user could receive an answer saying they are not able to vote if they say they are under 18. But if they input an answer of 30, they would get a second answer, such as information on their closest voting poll or another relevant piece of information.

The if else statement is going to allow for more freedom inside of your code. This makes it easier than ever before for you to handle whatever answer the user puts into the system, whether it is considered true or false. With this statement, the compiler will check the answer, and if it is seen as true for that particular one, it will execute that part of the code. But if not, it moves on to the second part of the code and executes that. You are able to expand on this, going down as many times as you would like if you want to have several different answers. Here is a good example of how you would be able to use the if else statement inside of Python:

```
age = int(input("Enter your age:"))
if (age <=18):
        print("You are not eligible for voting, try next election!")
else
        print("Congratulations! You are eligible to vote. Check out your local polling station to find out more information!)
print("Program ends")
```

With this example above, there are basically two options that you can use in the statement. If the user puts in their age as being 18 or younger, the first statement is the one that is going to come up. So on the screen, they are going to see the message "You are not eligible for voting, try next election!" But if the user puts in that they are 19 or above in age, they will see a different message that says: "Congratulations! You are eligible to vote. Check out your local polling station to find out more information!". This is a simple example that shows how the user will be able to put in any age that they want and the answer corresponding to their specific input is going to show up on the screen.

This one is a basic version of what you are able to do with the if else statement. This one just has one true, and one false answer and that is all that is on the statement. But there are times when you would like to have some options that the user can choose from, or you want there to be more than one true answer. For example, let's say that you would like to have the user put their favorite color. You could have five of the else statements with blue, red, yellow, green, and white. If the user puts in one of those five colors, the statement that is with that color will come up. Add in a break part that will catch all the other colors that your user may want to pick from so that an answer comes up no matter what answer they pick out.

The if else statements are able to add a lot of great things that you can use with your codes. It allows it to make a decision inside of the code based on the conditions that you set and the input that your user places into the code. It is nice to use the if else statements because you can better prepare for the various answers that your user will enter, no matter what they decide to answer, and you are all set to go.

The elif statements

One more conditional statement that we are going to talk about in this chapter is the elif statement. These are a bit different than the others, but they are nice to work with because they provide the user with a few choices that they can choose from. Each of your choices are going to have a statement or a part of the code that will execute based on the decision that your user decides to go with. If you are creating a game and would like to make sure that the user can pick from several options before going further on, the elif statement is the one that you should use. The syntax that you would want to use with the elif statement includes:

if expression1:
statement(s)
elif expression2:
statement(s)
elif expression3:
statement(s)
else:
statement(s)

This is the basic syntax that you will want to work with whenever you want to use the elif statements in Python. You can just add in some of the information that you want so that the user can see the choices and pick the numbers that they would like to go with it, or the statements that work with their choices. This is one that you will be able to expand out a bit as you need, and you can choose to have two or three options or twenty options based on what you would like to see happen with the elif statements.

Here, we are going to take some time to look at how the elif statement is able to work in your coding. With this option, we are going to list a few choices of pizzas that the user is able to pick from and the corresponding number that they are able to work with. You can always add in some more options as well, and we add in an else part that is able to catch all the other options or, in this option, that will allow them to get a drink instead of a pizza if they do not like the options that are presented to them. Let's take a look at how this would be written out in your Python compiler:

Print("Let's enjoy a Pizza! Ok, let's go inside Pizzahut!")
print("Waiter, Please select Pizza of your choice from the menu")
pizzachoice = int(input("Please enter your choice of Pizza:"))
if pizzachoice == 1:
         print('I want to enjoy a pizza napoletana')
elif pizzachoice == 2:
         print('I want to enjoy a pizza rustica')
elif pizzachoice == 3:
         print('I want to enjoy a pizza capricciosa')
else:

print("Sorry, I do not want any of the listed pizza's, please bring a Coca Cola for me.")

This is a pretty simple example of the elif statement and how you would be able to incorporate it into your codes. You can easily change this up to work with whatever program or game that you would like to create. The syntax, as you can see above, is offering the user a few options of pizzas that they are able to choose. When they are using the code, they will be able to pick the number that they would like and that corresponds to the pizza they want to go with. For example, if they would like to get the pizza napoletana, they would type in the number one. If they pick number one, they would see the answer "I want to enjoy a pizza napoletana" come up on their screen. This works for any of the numbers that they would choose on this option. With this one, we have even set it up so that the user can choose to just have a drink without a pizza if this is what they prefer.

The if statements are one of the best options for you to work with. They allow the code to come up with its own decisions based on the conditions that you set up in the beginning. You can make it as simple as the code just choosing to show a result when the user input is the same as your conditions, or you can add in some other parts to match up with the answers that the user places inside the code or with the choices that they want to make. There are many things that you are able to work with when using the conditional statements and you can make them as complicated or as simple as you would like.

Conclusion

Thank you for downloading *The Blueprint to Python Programming: A Beginners Guide to Everything You Need to Know to Get Started.*

The next step is to download the program and start writing some of your very own code. Since Python is a popular coding language and is great for beginners, it won't take long for you to get started on your first projects. This guidebook provided a few great examples that you can try out to get familiar with the system, but with the help of the knowledge you gained inside and the Python community, you will be writing great codes in no time. From learning how to write out the basic syntax in Python to working with conditional statements, operators, and variables, you are well on your way to being an expert in no time.

Finally, if you found this book useful in anyway, a review on Amazon is always appreciated!